Meet
John F. Kennedy

By Nancy Bean White

Step-Up Books   Random House

New York

List of Illustrations

Cover photograph by Georg Munker

Portrait of John F. Kennedy on spine of book and this page by Norman Rockwell
(Courtesy of The Saturday Evening Post, © 1963 by The Curtis Publishing Co.)

Title Page: President Kennedy with foreign students at the White House
(Abbie Rowe, National Parks Service)

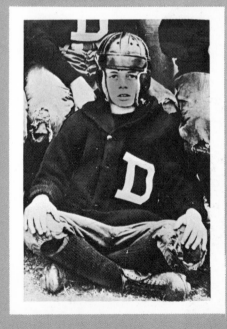

BOOK CLUB EDITION

End papers: Lower right-hand picture — *UPI*. All other pictures on end papers and other pictures in book not otherwise credited appear through the courtesy of the Kennedy family.

1

On November 22, 1963, a handsome young man rode into the city of Dallas, Texas. By his side sat his beautiful wife, all dressed in pink. It was a hot, sunny day in Dallas.

They rode in an open car. Their car
moved slowly. They smiled and
waved to the crowds along the
streets. People cheered. They were
glad these young people had come
to their city.

Suddenly the sound of three shots ripped the air. One shot hit the young man's neck. Another hit his head. He fell sideways into his wife's lap. Minutes later he was dead.

He was John Fitzgerald Kennedy, the 35th President of the United States. He had been shot and killed by an assassin.

Kennedy was President for only 2 years, 10 months, and 2 days. But people will always remember him.

People liked the young President. His thick brown hair would never stay in place. This amused them. When he smiled, they smiled with him. He had a good mind. He said things in a quick, sure way.

Only his family and friends knew his back almost always hurt him. John Kennedy was a brave man.

Being President is a hard job. And he worked very, very hard at it. Not all people agreed with what he did. Nor did all people agree with what he wanted to do. But most Americans cried when he died. And the rest of the world cried, too.

The world had liked his vigor and his energy. People liked the graceful ways he and his wife had brought to the White House. And young Americans had liked him most of all. They had felt that he was a very special friend.

2

No one knows why John Kennedy had so much energy. He may have been born with it. Or it may have come from the way he grew up.

He was the second of nine children born to Rose and Joseph Kennedy.

He was born on May 29, 1917, in Brookline, Massachusetts. Brookline is a town just outside the city of Boston. The Kennedys lived there.

As the family grew, they moved to other places. The big family always lived in big houses.

Her nine children kept Mrs. Rose Kennedy very busy. But she never got her four boys and five girls mixed up. She put all she knew about them on cards. This way she knew which ones had had measles and which ones mumps.

Mr. Joseph Kennedy's grandparents had come to Boston from Ireland. The family was poor. But Mr. Kennedy had worked hard.

He had done very well. He had become very rich. But he never let his children spend too much money. And he taught them to work hard. He wanted them to learn to do many things and to do them well. He taught them to try to be first in all things. He taught them to have fun, too. The children played games in 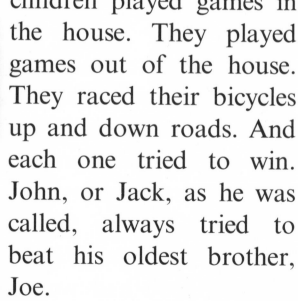 the house. They played games out of the house. They raced their bicycles up and down roads. And each one tried to win. John, or Jack, as he was called, always tried to beat his oldest brother, Joe.

And so did

Kathleen,

Rosemary,

Eunice,

Patricia,

Jean,

Robert,

and Edward.

When he grew up, Jack said he did not remember ever being unhappy as a child. He was often sick. But he loved to read books. He read many books about a goat named Billy Whiskers. He also read about the lives of heroes. All his life he kept his interest in books and heroes.

9

3

When Jack was 13 years old, he went away to school. He went to live in a boarding school in Connecticut. At first, he missed his family very much. But after he had been there a while he wrote to his mother: "It's O.K. now."

The next year Jack went to another fine boarding school. It was named Choate.

Jack went there for four years. He tried out for many sports teams.

He could swim well. He did not always study hard. But he did read books. And he could remember almost all that was in them.

He never made the top teams at Choate. His grades were not too good. But he was well liked by everyone. When he graduated, his class voted him "the most likely to succeed." They knew he would be first at something, someday.

When Jack left Choate he was ready for college. He went to Princeton. But he did not stay there long. He got sick. When he was well again he went to Harvard College. Jack's brother Joe was already at Harvard.

Joe was good at everything. Jack tried to keep up with him. Joe played football. Jack wanted to play, too. One day in a rough play he hurt his back. He did not know it then, but his back would never be really well again.

Jack also got sick trying to make the swimming team. He had been in bed with a bad cold. He was told he could not go to swimming practice. But he wanted so much to practice that he sneaked out of bed and went swimming. His cold became worse. He missed the team. And he did not feel well for the rest of the year.

4

While Jack was at Harvard, his father served as the United States' Ambassador to England. There was talk of war in Europe then. Jack wondered why countries went to war. He began to study about this. Then Harvard let Jack leave school to visit his father in London.

Jack went all over Europe with his father. He also went to many places by himself. He saw many things and he learned much.

Jack went back to Harvard. And soon after, war broke out in Europe. England and France declared war on Germany. Jack wrote a paper saying why he felt the war had started. The paper was so good it was made into a book. The book was called "Why England Slept."

When Jack graduated from Harvard, he graduated with honors. His father sent word to him. He said, "Two things I always knew about you. One, that you are smart. Two, that you are a swell guy."

Jack had won honors from Harvard. And from his father, too.

5

Jack graduated from Harvard in 1940. That summer the whole family went to their home in Hyannis Port, Massachusetts.

The Kennedys owned many houses. They could be at home in New York, in Florida, or in Massachusetts. But Jack liked their home in Hyannis Port best of all. There they played the games they all loved.

There they played tennis. They raced each other in boats. They played softball. They played touch football. The Kennedy girls were very good at that game. Sometimes they even beat their brothers.

They played games in the house, too. But often they just talked. They talked about war, politics, schools. They talked about movies, animals, sports. They talked about each other. Sometimes they all talked at once.

It was a noisy summer. It was so noisy Mrs. Kennedy could not find a quiet place to think. One day she shut herself in a big closet. It was the only quiet place she could find.

Every one of them remembered that summer. It was the last summer the whole family was together. Soon after, both Joe and Jack went into the United States Navy.

The doctors had found that Jack's back had never really healed. So Jack worked to make it strong. Then the Navy took him.

On December 7, 1941, Japanese airplanes flew over Pearl Harbor. They dropped bombs on American ships. The next day, the United States declared war on Japan. Three days later, Germany and Italy declared war on the United States. Joe and Jack were called to war by the Navy.

6

Jack was a lieutenant in the Navy. He was sent to the Solomon Islands in the Pacific Ocean. He was put in charge of a PT boat. A PT boat is small. She can sneak up on an enemy ship. She can blow it sky-high with a torpedo. Then she can get away quickly before she is caught.

Kennedy's boat was named PT 109. There was room on her for thirteen men.

The night of August 2, 1943, was a dark night. There was no moon. It was a good night for PT boats to hunt big Japanese ships.

The PT boats left their home base. It was so dark they were very bold. They went far away from the base. Far away from their own sister ships. And far away from any help.

PT 109 led three PT boats into the night.

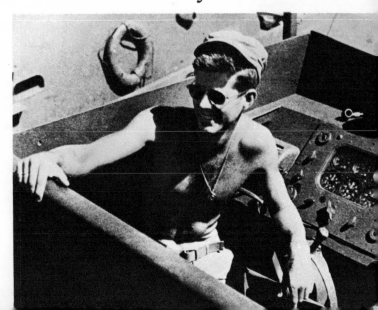

Kennedy steered his boat in the quiet water. His eyes searched for Japanese ships. Suddenly, out of the night came a huge shape. It was a Japanese destroyer. It was heading straight for PT 109. Jack spun the steering wheel fast.

He hoped one of PT 109's guns would get the ship. But it was too late. The destroyer hit PT 109. It cut her in half. Kennedy was thrown flat on his back. One half of PT 109 sank into the sea. The other half stayed afloat. Kennedy held on to this piece of boat with all his might.

Right away he counted his men. He hoped all thirteen would be there. Four men held on to the boat with him. That made five. He called into the dark. He got six answers. That made eleven. Two did not answer. They had been killed the very minute the boat was cut in two.

7

Kennedy swam out to help the other six men. It took three hours to get them all to the half-boat. Soon day came. But no help came. There was not a boat in sight.

They saw many islands all around.

But there were Japanese on them. There was one small island about three miles away. No one seemed to be on it. They wondered if they could swim that far.

Then they knew they would have to try. The rest of their boat was going down.

One man was too hurt to swim. Kennedy said he would pull him to land. He took the hurt man's life-jacket strap between his teeth. Then he began to swim. He and his men swam for five long hours. At last, they fell onto the beach.

After they were rested they looked for food. They found none. For five days they hid from the Japanese.

They swam out at night to near-by islands. But they found no friends. Soon they gave up hope.

Kennedy decided to make one last try. He took one man. They swam to one more island. There they found friendly people.

All eleven men were saved!

Lieutenant Kennedy was tired and sick when he got back to his base. He was thin. His back had been hurt again. The Navy gave him a medal for bravery. Then he was told he had to go home. Kennedy did not want to go. He told everyone he was fine. So they let him stay. He went back to sea. But soon his back began to hurt even more.

This time he could not hide it. He was sent to the United States. He was put in a hospital. And the doctors operated on his back.

Jack was still in the hospital when bad news came. His brother Joe had been killed in the war. Joe's airplane had exploded in the air.

8

The war went on. It was fought all over the world. But at last, on September 2, 1945, World War II came to an end. America and its allies won the war. But many young men had given their lives for the victory. Joseph P. Kennedy, Jr., had been one of these men.

Other men came home hurt and sick. Some of them would never be really well again. Jack Kennedy was one of these men. But Jack Kennedy did not think about being sick.

He thought about the kind of work he should do. He wondered if he should go into politics. Both of Jack's grandfathers were in politics in Massachusetts. His grandfather Patrick Joseph Kennedy had been a State Senator. Jack was named for his other grandfather. He was John Francis Fitzgerald. He had been a Mayor of Boston.

Both families had come to Boston from Ireland. Both grandfathers helped other Irish people who came to Boston. They helped them to find places to live. They helped them to find jobs.

All the Irish people in Boston knew Jack's grandfathers.

They knew Grandfather Fitzgerald so well they called him "Honey Fitz." They cheered when he sang the song "Sweet Adeline." Grandfather Fitzgerald loved that song. He would sing it without being asked.

Jack was shy. To become a politician he would have to shake many people's hands. He would have to make speeches. He would have to ask people to vote for him.

Jack was not sure he could do all this. But he decided he would try.

9

There are two great political parties in the United States. One is called the Republican party. The other is called the Democratic party.

The Kennedy family had always been Democrats. Jack had joined the Democratic party, too. He had joined by signing his name to the Democrats' list.

Now, Kennedy went to the Democrats. He wanted to be elected Representative. He wanted to speak for the people of Boston in the Congress.

Kennedy was young. There were older men who wanted the job. Kennedy had to show he could win more votes than the other men.

Kennedy would have to work very hard to get votes. Very few people knew who he was. So he went to every corner of his part of Boston.

He went to food stores, to flower shops, to train and bus stations. He stood on street corners. He rang doorbells. He talked to people anywhere he could find them.

At first, he was shy and scared. He still looked sick. He was not sure of what to say. He did not think he could win. But this only made him work harder.

His brothers and sisters held meetings to tell people about him. His friends from school and his friends from the war came to help him, too. They made signs. They wrote letters, stamped them, and mailed them to voters. They worked day and night.

The voters of Boston liked these busy young people. They especially liked John Kennedy. They thought he would work hard for them in Washington. On voting day the voters chose Kennedy.

All the Kennedys were happy. Grandfather Fitzgerald was so happy he danced a jig on a table. And he sang "Sweet Adeline."

10

Representative Kennedy went to Washington in January, 1947. He was only 29 years old. He looked so young, the older Congressmen did not take him very seriously. One of them called him "Laddie."

But soon they began to listen when he talked. He seemed to know a great deal. He was not afraid to say what he thought. And he was willing to learn. Wherever he went he asked questions.

Kennedy traveled a lot. He traveled in this country and in many other countries. One time he went all the way around the world. But he never forgot the people of Boston. He always tried to get new laws that would help them. The people of Boston sent him to Washington three times as their Representative. After he had been one of Boston's Representatives for six years he wanted a bigger job.

He wanted to be a Senator. Senators work for all the people in a state. A Republican had the Senate seat that Kennedy could try for. His name was Henry Cabot Lodge, Jr.

Lodge had been elected a Senator from Massachusetts three times. He wanted to be elected again.

Lodge was well liked by the voters. The Republicans were sure Kennedy could not beat Lodge.

Again, Kennedy's big family came to help him. His brother Robert ran the office. The girls rang doorbells. His mother gave tea parties. His father gave advice and money to help pay the bills.

And Jack himself never stopped running. He went all over Massachusetts asking people to vote for him.

The biggest surprise of that election year, 1952, was that Kennedy beat Lodge.

11

Soon after Senator Kennedy got back to Washington, he went to call on a beautiful young lady. Her name was Jacqueline Bouvier. Her hair was dark and her smile was wide. When she smiled, her eyes sparkled. The Senator liked her voice. It was soft and quiet.

Jacqueline Bouvier had been born in New York. But she spoke French, Italian, and Spanish, as well as English. She liked to draw and paint. She liked to read books.

Kennedy had met her the year before. He liked her then. But he was busy getting elected. He had no time to see her. Now he was back in Washington. They could eat dinner and go to a movie. Jack loved movies. They both liked books. So they gave each other books for presents. When Jack was out of town he telephoned her.

On September 12, 1953, Jacqueline Bouvier and Jack Kennedy were married.

All who were at the wedding said the bride was very beautiful. The Senator was happy. No one could tell from his face that his back was hurting again.

Soon after the wedding, Kennedy found it hard to walk. The doctors gave him crutches. He hated the crutches. They got in his way. They kept him from moving fast. And they did not do him any good. His back still hurt. He asked the doctors to operate on his back again. They told him they were afraid to operate. He might die.

12

The doctors waited for a year.
Then, at last, they operated on
Kennedy's back. They had to
operate two times. For months
and months he lay on his back.
He was in great pain. His wife,
Jackie, sat by him day and night.

He could not take care of much
of his Senate work from his bed.
But nothing could stop him from
thinking.

He thought about heroes and leaders. He saw that real heroes are men who stand up bravely for what they think.

He decided to write a book about such men. He called it "Profiles in Courage." Did John Kennedy wonder if he could be as good and as brave as the men he wrote about? He probably did.

At last the day came when he could throw away his crutches. And right away he flew back to Washington. He had been sick for more than a year.

The Senators had missed him. They all stood up and clapped when he walked into the Senate.

Senator Kennedy always kept the door to his office open. People could walk in when they needed him. And he took care of their needs right away.

In the Senate he always worked hard for the things he believed in. He did not think he could work for too many things at one time. He picked those ideas and laws about which he cared most.

He studied the laws to get his facts straight. Then he made strong speeches about them. Sometimes he made the other Senators very cross. But he knew how to make them laugh, too. One way or the other, he often won his point.

MASSACHUSETTS

1956
DEMOCRATIC
NATIONAL
CONVENTION

1956
DEMOCRATIC
NATIONAL
CONVENTION

OUR CHOICE

13

Early in 1956 the world began to think about the next President of the United States. A President would be elected that year. Republicans and Democrats had been thinking about it for some time.

A President and Vice-President are elected every four years. So every four years each party chooses the men it wants to be its candidates. To do this each party holds a big meeting, called a convention.

No one building will hold everyone who belongs to a party. So each party chooses a few men and women from each state to go to its convention. They are called delegates.

In 1956 the Republican delegates met in San Francisco. They chose President Dwight D. Eisenhower to run again for President. And they chose Richard M. Nixon to run again for Vice-President.

The Democratic delegates met in Chicago. They chose Adlai Stevenson as their candidate for President. Then they talked about men who might be Vice-President. Many delegates talked about John Kennedy as a candidate.

Kennedy had been a Senator for four years. He was still young to be Vice-President. He was only 39 years old. But people had seen that the voters liked him.

Kennedy's friends went to work. They asked delegates to vote for him.

When it came time to vote, two men were ahead of all the others. They were Senator John Kennedy and Senator Estes Kefauver. But when the vote was in, Kefauver had won.

Kennedy was disappointed. But he smiled. He was a good sport. Those who were watching television saw this. And that day, many people liked John Kennedy.

14

Kennedy worked hard for the Democratic candidates. But the Democrats lost. Eisenhower and Nixon were elected. They would be the President and Vice-President for the next four years.

Now Kennedy turned again to his work in the Senate.

The years between 1956 and 1958 were good ones for Kennedy. They were good in the Senate and good at home. In 1957, a little girl was born to Senator and Mrs. Kennedy. They named her Caroline. But her father called her "Buttons."

Three of Caroline's first words were "Daddy," "airplane," "car." Her Daddy hurried everywhere. By 1958 people all over the country were talking about the young Senator. And some were even working to make him President.

Kennedy himself was not sure he should try to be President. Then in 1958 he was re-elected Senator from Massachusetts.

He won by a great many votes. This made him think that maybe he could be a candidate for President.

And it made a lot of other people think so, too. All across the country people began to talk about young Kennedy.

Then the whole Kennedy family went to work. Robert was boss. Jean's husband, Steve, was head of a "Kennedy for President" office in Washington. Edward worked out West. Patricia and her husband worked in California. Eunice and her husband worked in Illinois. Watching over it all was their father, Mr. Joseph Kennedy.

John and Jackie started going around the country. They found he was a long way from being chosen by the Democratic party as their candidate. And he was a very long way from being elected President.

15

One thing that stood in the way of Kennedy's being chosen a candidate was his religion. He was a Catholic. The United States had elected Presidents for 171 years. But Americans had never elected a Catholic President. Many were afraid to do so.

Kennedy said America was founded by men who came here to worship God in their own ways. "This is the kind of America I believe in," he said. Kennedy said he was a good Catholic. Other men were Jews. Or Protestants. He said people should vote for the best man, no matter what his religion. Kennedy had to get people in many states to believe this. Only then would they choose delegates who would vote for him at the Democratic convention.

One of the states Kennedy went to was West Virginia. Most of the people there were Protestants. They did not know if they wanted a Catholic President.

Kennedy hoped he could win in West Virginia. This would prove people would vote for a Catholic.

Kennedy told the people of West Virginia it was not fair to hold a man's religion against him.

He said the United States had asked Catholics to fight and die in the war. His brother Joe had died. He said if our country asks Catholics to fight and die it should let Catholics be elected, too.

Kennedy talked to the people of West Virginia about their own needs, too. Their need for jobs. For food. He said that as President he would try to help them.

West Virginians believed him.

By July, 1960, many delegates of many states had decided to vote for Kennedy. But he could not be sure he would win. Other men wanted to be the Democratic candidate for President, too.

16

A convention is like a circus. Delegates come from north, south, east, and west. Some wear cowboy hats. Some wear long string neckties. They are tall, short, fat and thin. But they all love politics. And they are all excited. They have come to name a Presidential candidate.

Each candidate has his own group of followers. They wear big buttons and crazy hats. They sing songs, wave signs, and march up and down.

All of this makes a lot of noise. A chairman calls for quiet. He bangs a big gavel. Often he has to bang it for ten minutes to be heard.

The Democrats met in July, 1960. When they began voting, there was hardly a sound in the hall. There were five men for whom they could vote. Two of these men might keep Kennedy from winning. They were Senator Lyndon B. Johnson and Adlai Stevenson. But they did not stop Kennedy. He won on the very first vote.

The crowds cheered. The bands played. Robert went to meet his brother. Then they went to the cheering convention hall.

Now Kennedy had to choose a Vice-President to run with him. Once he had said Johnson would be a good President. Now he wanted the best man he could find. The Vice-President would take over if something happened to the President. So he asked Johnson to run with him as Vice-President. Johnson said yes.

Then Kennedy spoke to the convention. He said, "My call is to the young in heart. Give me your help, your hand, your voice, your vote." The crowd cheered.

Ten days went by. Then the Republicans held their convention. They chose Richard M. Nixon to be their candidate for President.

17

Richard Nixon would be a very hard man to beat. He was the Vice-President. The country knew him. Like Kennedy, he was young. But many people thought he would know more about how to run the country than Kennedy.

Senator Kennedy did not agree.

Now, he used every talent he had. He did everything he had done before to win. And more. He hardly slept. He almost never stopped to eat. He visited as many as 20 places a day. He told the people that the country must not stand still. He said it had to move faster, farther, sooner.

Kennedy read. He telephoned. He asked questions. And he answered questions. He debated many questions on television with Vice-President Nixon. He was sure of himself. He knew a lot about everything. Soon people began to say he was not too young. He knew just as much as Mr. Nixon.

The cheers for him grew louder. The crowds grew bigger, It seemed that Kennedy might even win. But no one knew for sure.

Each voter asked himself: Did Kennedy want the country to go too fast? Was he old enough? Did it matter that he was a Catholic?

Would he keep his word about what he said he would do?

On November 7, the country voted. Many people answered these questions in Kennedy's favor. He was elected President. The vote was close. Many people had voted for Nixon. But it was a great victory for the young Senator from Massachusetts.

18

The next morning, he spoke to the world. Jackie stood at his side. He said only a few words. At the very end he said, "So now my wife and I prepare for a new administration and for a new baby."

Soon after, a baby boy was born to Jacqueline and John Kennedy. They named him John Fitzgerald Kennedy, Jr. His father called him John-John.

The days after Kennedy won were busy days at Hyannis Port. In one way it was just like old times. Yet there was a difference. Now, even his best friends called him Mr. President. Secret Service men guarded him closely.

In January the Kennedys moved to the White House. Caroline took her pets. They were Charlie, the dog, Robin, the canary, and Tom, the kitten.

Mrs. Kennedy made the White House feel just like home. She built a brand-new kitchen. Then she painted the family living room yellow. And she set the President's rocking chair by the fireplace.

Then she turned to the rooms downstairs. Visitors came to look at these. Here she wanted the White House to show its own history.

Once she had visited another country. She had seen that everything in the President's house there had a link with the past. "I thought the White House should be like that," she said.

So she set out to find very old chairs and tables. She looked for dishes that had been used by other Presidents. She even found wall-paper that was 126 years old.

That year more Americans came to visit the White House than ever before.

19

President Kennedy loved being President. But there were little things that were hard for him to get used to. He did not like being guarded. He was used to moving fast. Sometimes he moved so fast in a crowd the Secret Service men lost him.

And he kept forgetting that as President he had to be first to go into a room. He was used to holding the door for his wife.

President Kennedy thought his wife was a wonderful First Lady. He was very proud of her. He knew hers was not a job she would have chosen. She was shy and quiet. She liked quiet times at home with just the two of them or a few friends. He knew that it was hard for her to get used to always being looked at.

She wanted to bring up Caroline and John-John like other children. She tried to do this. But they both knew that people would always want to look at their children. People stood outside the White House gates. They stood all day just to see them play in the garden.

People loved to see pictures of Caroline and John-John with their father, in his office.  They wanted to hear about the times he took them for swims and out to buy candy. They talked about Caroline in her mother's shoes. About John-John's hair cut. They noted that the President did not like to wear a winter coat. He almost never wore a hat. People loved Mrs. Kennedy's dresses. Many women copied them.

The Kennedy family gave the world so much to see, to think about, to admire. And they were loved because of it.

20

The President of the United States lives in the White House. He works there, too. From his office window, Kennedy could see Caroline and John-John in the garden.

Often they came in to see him for a minute or two. But that was all. He could never be away from his work for long. It was with him day and night.

Kennedy loved his wife and children. But he loved his country, too. He was doing what he had asked other Americans to do when he became President.

"Ask not what your country can do for you," he had said. "Ask what you can do for your country."

The President felt the country was ready for change. He wanted the country to cross new frontiers. So he called his time the New Frontier.

The New Frontier needed new thinking. He called in thinkers to help him. Many he called were teachers. President Kennedy knew teachers could study well. They knew how to get facts.

Kennedy never stopped asking questions. He wanted to know every fact. He was quick to remember what he heard. He liked to hear from people who did not agree with him. He liked it best if an argument was as good as his own, or better.

Kennedy always listened with great care. When the time came to decide what to do, he decided quickly. Sometimes what he decided to do was wrong. When that happened, he quickly took the blame for being wrong.

The United States was strong when Kennedy became President. But he asked Congress for new laws to make it even stronger.

He wanted a law to help old people who were sick. He wanted all people in the land to be treated in a fair way. Not just those with white skins.

He called to the young in heart. He asked them to teach people in poor countries. He said there were many things they wanted to know. How to build roads, how to read and write, or how to get rid of bugs.

Kennedy had been in a war. He wanted to keep peace. He talked to the leaders of other countries. He even talked to leaders who were not always friendly to the United States. He put in a special wire so he could talk to Nikita Khrushchev in Russia. It was called "the hot line."

Kennedy said the United States should be strong. But he knew other countries wanted to be strong, too. Some countries were testing bigger and bigger bombs. He felt this was bad for the whole world. He talked with the heads of other countries. He asked them to sign a treaty with the United States. The treaty said the signers would stop testing big bombs. It was signed by 102 countries.

Now Kennedy thought all people could be safer. President Kennedy cared most about this.

21

Kennedy was not able to make all the changes he wanted to make. He learned a whole country cannot move as fast as one man. Big changes take time. Kennedy hoped the country would give him this time. He hoped the people would re-elect him President at the end of his first four years. He believed they would.

Kennedy felt it was important for a President to see the people and for the people to see him.

He went to Dallas in November of 1963. He knew then that not all of the people there liked him. But he asked that he and Mrs. Kennedy ride in an open car. That way he and the people could see each other.

And so it was that President John F. Kennedy was shot.

Everyone will long remember his young good looks. His ready smile. His quick step. He was a man on the move. A brave man.

He looked for the paths to move ahead. Then he stepped out in front of his country and its people.

He said follow me to the end of the road. And we will seek out greatness.

He was struck down long before we could see what lay at the end of his road. But for a moment we caught his step. And when he turned, we smiled.

After President Kennedy Was Killed

Right after President Kennedy was killed, the Dallas police arrested a man named Lee Harvey Oswald. The police believed Oswald had killed the President. But they were not able to find out from him if he had done it or why he had done it. For Oswald himself was killed before he could tell what he knew.

President Lyndon Johnson thought the world should know all the facts about President Kennedy's murder. He asked seven men to find out everything they could about it.

Nearly one year later, on September 24, 1964, the seven men gave President Johnson a huge book. In it was everything they had learned about the murder.

The things they had learned made the seven men sure it was Lee Harvey Oswald who had killed President Kennedy. They believed Oswald was not in his right mind when he did it.